The Lord Jesus

THE LORD JESUS

by *Carol Savage*

ILLUSTRATED BY GIL MIRET

THE SEABURY PRESS

Greenwich, Connecticut

THE LORD JESUS was prepared for the Department of Christian Education of the National Council of the Protestant Episcopal Church at the direction of General Convention as part of the Church's Teaching for closely graded church schools.

Contents

Jesus Calls the Fishermen   9
Jesus Teaches His Friends to Pray   13
Jesus Answers a Question   17
The Lost Sheep   21
Jesus and the Children   23
An Angel Visits Mary   25
Jesus Is Born   28
The Wise Men Visit Jesus   32
Jesus Heals a Blind Man   36
Jesus Visits Zacchaeus   40
Jesus Comes to Jerusalem   45
Jesus Dies and Lives Again   49
Breakfast on the Shore   57
Jesus Sends His Spirit   65

The Lord Jesus

Jesus Calls the Fishermen

ONE morning, a man stood on the shore of the Sea of Galilee. The water slapped softly among the pebbles at His feet. Warm sunshine streamed down, and, not far away, fishing boats rocked gently on the calm sea.

The man was Jesus. All His life, He had lived in Nazareth with Mary, His mother, and Joseph, the carpenter. Not long ago, Jesus had left His home. Taking nothing with Him, He had gone out to teach God's love to the world.

At first, Jesus traveled alone. Wherever He went, down dusty roads, over hills, through valleys, to big towns and tiny villages, He walked on foot. Sometimes He stayed with friends. Sometimes He slept in the open, under the stars.

9

When He came to a town, Jesus talked to people. Gathered round Him, they would listen, astonished at the wise things He said. "Isn't this Joseph's son?" they asked each other, "the carpenter from Nazareth?" They could hardly believe their ears.

On this particular morning at Galilee, a crowd of people had followed Jesus down to the shore. They pressed close about Him, waiting to hear Him

10

speak. Looking about for a place to sit, Jesus saw two fishing boats pulled up to the land. The boats belonged to Simon Peter, his brother Andrew, and their partners, James and John. The four men were knee-deep in the water nearby, washing their nets after a long night's fishing.

These men were fine fishermen. They knew where the fish lurked in the deep, dark water.

Now Jesus asked Peter to push his boat a little away from the land so He could sit in it to speak to the crowd.

Jesus' voice carried strong and clear across the water. When He had finished speaking, He turned to the four fishermen who had stopped washing their nets to listen.

"Follow me," He said. "I have work for you to do."

Peter and Andrew, James and John, left everything they had behind them. They left their boats, their homes, and their friends. They simply followed Jesus as He walked away.

Jesus Teaches His Friends to Pray

WHEN Jesus said "Follow me," Peter, Andrew, James, and John left all they had to go with Him. Jesus called other men, too. Like the four fishermen, they left their homes to be with Him. Soon there were twelve men who followed Jesus everywhere. They were His close friends, His disciples.

To be a disciple was not easy. Sometimes it meant giving up comfortable things—warm beds, good food, money, friends. But the disciples went with Jesus gladly. They followed Him from place to place, sailed with Him from one town to another on the shores of the Sea of Galilee, or sat with Him on the hillsides as He spoke to the hundreds of people who came to hear Him. Jesus told stories the disciples never forgot, stories of God's love and hope for His people.

13

It was a busy life, for Jesus never stayed long in one place. When people asked Him to stay with them for a little while, He would say, "God's message will not wait. I must take it to another town. That is what I came to do."

To the sick, the hurt, and the helpless, Jesus was always gentle. He had the power to make well again those who were sick. Day after day these people came to Jesus, and He healed them.

There were times when Jesus wanted to be by Himself, to rest and pray. Then He would go to a quiet place.

One day, while Jesus was praying, His disciples came to Him. "Teach us how to pray as you do," they asked.

And Jesus said, "When you pray, say this:

Our Father, who art in heaven,
Hallowed be thy Name.
Thy kingdom come. Thy will be done,
On earth as it is in heaven.
Give us this day our daily bread.
And forgive us our trespasses, As we for-
    give those who trespass against us.
And lead us not into temptation, But
    deliver us from evil."

The disciples learned their Lord's prayer, and taught it to others. Later, Jesus' followers added these words to the prayer: "For thine is the kingdom, and the power, and the glory, for ever and ever. Amen."

Jesus Answers a Question

IN THE days when Jesus lived in Palestine, the road from Jerusalem to Jericho was a lonely, dangerous place. Robbers hid in the hills, waiting to spring out on travelers, to steal their money and all they had. At night the little foxes came out to bark at the moon.

Jesus knew the Jericho road, and one day He told a story about it to a man who asked Him a difficult question. "I know that God says I must love my neighbor as myself," the man said. "But tell me, Teacher, who *is* my neighbor?"

"Listen," Jesus said. "A man was going down the Jericho road. On the way, robbers came out of the hills and jumped on him. They beat him, took his clothes and his money, and left him lying in the dirt, badly hurt and helpless.

"Now soon after the robbers had gone, another man came down the road from Jerusalem. This man was a priest and much respected. He saw the wounded man, but he did not stop. Instead, he hurried by on the other side of the road.

"Later, a second man came along. He, like the priest, was thought to be a fine fellow. But he did not stop either. When he came to the place where the traveler lay, he went on as fast as he could.

"Finally, a third man came down the road. This man had journeyed a long way. He was a stranger, from the land of Samaria. Seeing the man lying in the road, the stranger took pity on him at once. He left his horse, and ran over to see what he could do. He took a cloth from his pack, bandaged the man's wounds, and gave him a drink. Then he lifted him onto the horse, and continued his journey.

19

"Before long, they came to an inn. The stranger from Samaria carried the injured man inside and took care of him.

"The next day, the Samaritan called the inn-keeper into the room. He gave him some money and said, 'Take good care of this poor fellow. See to it that he gets everything he needs. If you spend more money than I have given you, I will repay you on my way back, for I shall pass this way again.'

"And the Samaritan went on his way."

When Jesus finished His story, He looked at the man who had asked, "Who is my neighbor?" "You have heard this story," He said. "Now, what do you think? Which of these three men was a neighbor to the man robbed on the Jericho road?"

The answer came quickly. "Why, the one who helped, of course."

And Jesus said, "You are quite right. Now you go and do as he did."

The Lost Sheep

ONCE Jesus heard a group of men muttering and complaining about His friends. "What kind of a man is He?" one asked. "He has friends that you and I wouldn't speak to, but He even eats His dinner with them."

Jesus went up to the men and said:

"Listen to me. . . . Suppose a shepherd owns a hundred sheep. He is a good shepherd, but one of his sheep strays away from the others. It wanders off into the hills where the wild wolf prowls. It is all alone, lost and afraid.

"Now if you were that shepherd, what would you do?

"Surely, you would leave the other sheep safe in the pasture and go searching for your one lost lamb. That is what a good shepherd does. When the shepherd finds his sheep, he is glad—he rejoices. He picks it up and carries it home. Then he calls to his friends and neighbors. 'Look all of you,' he cries. 'I have found my sheep, the one that was lost. I have brought him safely home!'

"I tell you this," Jesus said. "The shepherd rejoices when he finds his lost sheep, and God rejoices when one of His people is rescued. There is more joy in heaven over one person who is truly sorry for the wrong he has done, than for ninety-nine people who do not need to be sorry. God goes out to search for those who are lost. This is what I came to do."

Jesus and the Children

GREAT crowds used to gather whenever word went out that Jesus was coming.

One day some mothers and fathers brought their children to see Jesus. They tried to get near Him, but the children were small, everyone else was big—they could not get through the crowd. So the mothers and fathers took their children by the hand. Squeezing between people, pushing and shoving, they made a path for the children and managed to get quite close to Jesus.

But some of the disciples came up and tried to send them away.

"Can't you see that Jesus is busy?" they scolded. "Get along . . . " And they tried to make the parents take their children out of the way.

Jesus saw what was happening. He stopped talking to the older people and looked angrily at His disciples. "Stop!" He said. "Don't ever send children away. Let them come to me. To such belongs the kingdom of God."

The children came and stood beside Jesus. Then He blessed them, touching them with His hands.

An Angel Visits Mary

WHEN Mary, Jesus' mother, heard of the wonderful things her Son was doing, she remembered the day she had learned He was to be born.

Mary was a young woman then. Soon she would marry Joseph, the carpenter, and go to live with him.

One day, not long before Mary and Joseph were married, God sent His angel Gabriel to Mary. The angel came to tell her that she had been chosen to be the mother of God's Son.

Mary was greatly troubled. She did not know why God should send His angel, and she did not understand the words He spoke. She was frightened.

"Do not be afraid, Mary," the angel said. "You are to be the mother of a son. He will be very great, the King of God's people forever." Then he told Mary that she must name her son Jesus.

Mary was astonished. "I am to be a mother?" she asked the angel. "How can this be?"

"With God, nothing is impossible," the angel replied. "Your son will be born. He will be called holy . . . the Son of God."

In wonder Mary listened to the angel, and she believed him.

"I am the Lord's," she said. "I serve Him gladly. Let this happen to me, just as you have said."

And when Mary finished speaking, the angel left her and returned to God.

Jesus Is Born

MARY and Joseph were going to Bethlehem.

It was a long way to go. Mary rode on the back of a donkey, but Joseph trudged by her side on foot.

They traveled for several days, but when they finally came to Bethlehem, weary from their journey, they could not find a place to stay. The town was so crowded, they were turned away from every door. In all of Bethlehem, no one could offer them a resting place, and there was no room for them at the inn.

At last they found shelter in the stable of the inn. Joseph tied the donkey to a post, and Mary lay down to rest in the straw near the gentle animals.

While they were there, Jesus was born. Because there was no bed for her baby, Mary wrapped Him warmly and laid Him in a manger.

In the fields outside the town that night, shepherds kept watch over their sheep. When Jesus was born, an angel appeared before them, and the night was filled with a glorious light. The shepherds covered their faces. They were afraid.

The angel spoke to them. "Do not be afraid," he said. "I bring you good news—good news of great joy to all people. For a Saviour, Christ the Lord, is born today. This shall be a sign for you to know Him: you will find a baby lying in a manger."

Suddenly the shepherds saw angels all about, filling the air with song:

> "Glory to God in the highest,
> And on earth peace,
> Good will toward men."

When the angels had gone away, the shepherds looked at each other in great excitement. "Let us go to Bethlehem!" they cried. "We must see what has happened . . . " And they ran into the town.

Just as the angel had said, the shepherds found Mary and Joseph in the stable, and there was the baby, asleep in a manger. They were amazed.

The shepherds went back to their sheep, talking of all they had seen and heard, and praising God.

Mary watched over her newborn boy; quietly thinking, quietly wondering.

The Wise Men Visit Jesus

ON THE very night Jesus was born, a bright new star appeared in the sky. Far away in another country, wise men saw the star. They believed it proclaimed the birth of a King.

Eagerly, the wise men ordered their camels made ready for a long journey. Then each selected a gift to take to the new King, and—dressed in their finest robes—they mounted their camels and set off to find Him.

Over the deserts and mountains they traveled, until they came to Jerusalem. When they arrived, they asked, "Where is He that is born King of the Jews? We have seen His star, and have come to worship Him."

Now King Herod lived in Jerusalem. He was a cruel man. Everyone feared him. When he heard that the wise men had come, asking about the birth of a new king, he was alarmed and angry. He asked questions and was told that long ago it had been said that the Holy Child would be born in Bethlehem.

Herod was sly and clever. He called for the wise men. He asked them about the star. Then he told them to go to Bethlehem. "When you have found the Child," he said, "come back to Jerusalem and tell me so that I, too, may go and worship Him."

But in his heart, Herod planned to kill the Child.

The wise men started out for Bethlehem. Suddenly, the star they had seen at its rising went before them. In great excitement they followed it until they came to the place where Mary and Joseph and the Child Jesus were staying.

Joyfully, the wise men hurried inside. When they saw Jesus, they fell on their knees and worshiped Him. They brought out their gifts—gold, and jars of precious perfume. The wise men laid these treasures before the Holy Child.

They did not return to Jerusalem. Warned not to tell Herod they had found the Christ Child, the wise men went back to their own country by another road.

Herod never found Jesus, for one night Joseph took his family and went away into the land of Egypt. There they stayed until King Herod died.

Later, Mary and Joseph returned to Nazareth with Jesus. Joseph worked at his carpentry, and Mary cared for her Son.

The years went by; Jesus grew to be a man. He worked with Joseph until God called to Him. Then the young carpenter put aside His tools. Jesus of Nazareth set out to do the work God had given Him.

Jesus Heals a Blind Man

IN A town called Jericho lived a poor blind man named Bartimaeus. Because he could not see, Bartimaeus could do no work. Instead, he sat under a tree by the side of the road in his old coat, holding out his hand to the people going by, hoping they would give him a penny.

Sometimes they did; often they did not.

Blind Bartimaeus knew the shape of things, for he could feel them with his hands. Hard, smooth stones; furry animals; soft, juicy fruit. He could feel the sun on his back or the rain on his face; he could hear the wind's song, and the bird's call, and the squeak of the saddles on the camels' backs as they plodded slowly past him into the town. But for Bartimaeus, the day was as dark as the night, and he was lonely.

One day as Bartimaeus sat under the tree, he heard the sound of many footsteps. People hurried past, laughing and talking.

"Who is coming?" Bartimaeus asked them. "Someone is coming. I cannot see Him; tell me who it is."

They told him it was Jesus of Nazareth.

Bartimaeus longed to see Jesus. Raising his face, he cried in a loud voice, "Jesus, have pity on me."

People told Bartimaeus to be still and not trouble Jesus with his crying and calling. But Bartimaeus only called out louder than before, holding out his hands, "Jesus, have pity on me."

Jesus heard him.

He stopped and said, "Bring him to me."

Some men took Bartimaeus by the hands, and he jumped up. His old coat fell to the ground and

he left it there. They led him to Jesus, saying, "Cheer up. He is calling you."

Jesus said, "What do you want me to do for you?"

Bartimaeus answered, "Jesus, open my eyes so I may see."

Jesus reached out and touched the eyes of the blind man standing before him. "Your faith has made you well," He said.

Suddenly Bartimaeus saw Jesus; he saw the sky, and the grass, and the faces of the people. The day was no longer as dark as the night, and Bartimaeus was no longer lonely.

When Jesus turned and started up the road, Bartimaeus followed Him.

Jesus Visits Zacchaeus

JERICHO was a busy city, full of noisy excitement. Roman soldiers paraded by, women called, children ran about, shopkeepers shouted their wares. Camels swung through the streets, laden with spices and oils and bright-dyed cloth from the east.

There was one man in Jericho whom nobody

liked. His name was Zacchaeus, and he was a tax collector.

When Zacchaeus collected the tax money, he often took more than he should. That was one of the reasons nobody liked him. Another was that Zacchaeus worked for the Romans. So even though Zacchaeus was rich and important, had a fine house and servants, he had very few friends. People never came to see him unless they had to.

Jesus came to Jericho on His way to Jerusalem. The streets were lined with people, for word of His coming had spread like wildfire through the town. Everyone was curious to see Him. Zacchaeus was curious too.

What sort of man is Jesus, he wondered? Zacchaeus decided to see for himself.

He left his house and hurried to a spot where Jesus would be sure to pass.

Now Zacchaeus was a small man. He found he could see nothing over the heads of the people already waiting in the street. He tried to push to the front of the crowd, but he was elbowed out of the way.

In his eagerness to see Jesus, Zacchaeus ran on ahead. His sandals slapped the cobblestones, and his wide robe flowed out behind as he hurried along. Not far away, he came to a tree, its branches stretching out over the street. Zacchaeus caught hold of a branch and swung himself off the ground. Up he climbed till he was above the crowd. Breathless, he waited and watched. He was only just in time.

Down the road came Jesus. Zacchaeus knew Him at once.

Jesus was surrounded by His disciples and many men and women from Jericho. When they reached the tree, Jesus stopped. He looked up at the little man peering down out of the branches. Then He spoke.

"Zacchaeus," He said. "Zacchaeus, hurry and come down. I am going to stay in your house to-day."

Zacchaeus was astonished. No one ever came to his house. Yet of all the people in Jericho that day,

Jesus had chosen him—the small, hated tax collector.

Almost unbelieving, he climbed down from the tree. Joyfully, he made Jesus welcome, and together they started off for Zacchaeus' house.

Others were surprised, too; surprised and angry.

"Surely Jesus doesn't mean to spend the day in that man's house," they said. "He's a tax collector for the Romans . . . No decent Jew would take a job like that. . . ."

Zacchaeus heard them muttering. Just outside the door of his house he stopped and spoke.

"It is true, I am a rich man . . . But Lord," he said to Jesus, "for your sake I will give half of my money away to the poor. And if I have taken more than I should, I will pay it back—four times over."

"This is a good day for you, Zacchaeus," Jesus said to the tax collector. Then He turned to the angry crowd. "I came to look for and save people who are lost," He said. "Zacchaeus is one of God's people, just as you are. I came for his sake as much as I came for yours."

Zacchaeus opened the door. Jesus went inside.

Jesus Comes to Jerusalem

ONE spring day, Jesus stood on a hill looking across at the bright and shining city of Jerusalem. Before Him, a road wound down the hill, through gardens and orchards. Not far away, the great city glittered in the sun.

Jesus knew that to take the road to Jerusalem was to take the road to danger, even death. He knew that angry men waited for Him there, plotting to destroy Him.

Jesus had spoken of the danger to His disciples and friends. They had not understood or believed Him. Now the time had come. He would enter the city and face His enemies.

All His disciples were with Jesus that day. His twelve closest friends. Many other people, too, were going with Him into the city. Their hopes were high. Surely, they thought, Jesus would be recognized as King. All He had done and said made them feel that something tremendous was going to happen. They were bursting with excitement.

Jesus asked two of His disciples to bring Him a young donkey from a village nearby. It was a little animal which had never been ridden before. Staring about with enormous eyes, it flicked long ears and waited on tiny, neat hooves. The disciples threw their coats over its back, for it wore no saddle, and Jesus mounted. With a shake of its head, the little donkey started off.

People crowded the road in front of Jesus; they followed after Him. Some of them tossed their coats down for Jesus to ride over; others cut branches from the trees and waved them in the air, shouting with joy. Singing, laughing, and cheering, the procession moved toward the city.

Hearing the noise, people in Jerusalem came out to meet them. They added their voices to the cries of the disciples. "Hosanna!" they all shouted. "Praise God. . . . Blessed is He who comes in the Name of the Lord!" Jesus was their King; He was going to Jerusalem; He would set them free. No wonder they cried "Hosanna!"

Gaily, joyfully, the procession descended the hill and passed through the city gates. Only Jesus, riding quietly on the back of the humble donkey, knew what dark days lay ahead.

Jesus Dies and Lives Again

JESUS was in terrible danger. Every day that passed, every hour He spent in the great city of Jerusalem brought the danger closer. Behind the palace doors, in the courtyards of the great Temple, His enemies plotted and whispered their plans. They were powerful men, but they were afraid of Jesus, and they were determined to get rid of Him.

Just the same, Jesus went about the city openly, speaking God's word, doing God's work. He knew what He must do; He knew what would happen. Soon He would show how deeply God loved the world.

Several days went by. Then, Jesus gathered His twelve disciples together. Upstairs, in the house of a friend, they sat down to eat their last supper together.

As they were eating, Jesus took bread and blessed it; He broke it into pieces, giving some to each disciple. Then He took a cup of wine, and when He had given thanks, He passed it to them in turn, and they drank from it.

In that upstairs room, Jesus talked to His friends. He told them many things that night, things they did not understand until later.

"In a little while," He said to them, "you will not see me any more. But you must not be troubled, or grieve for me. I am going to God, my father. In a little while I will be back with you again."

The disciples were puzzled. "What do you mean?" they asked. "Are you going away? You say you are leaving us, but will come back again. ... What do you mean?"

"Some day soon, you will understand," Jesus said to them. "You will know that I have come back, that I am with you. Do not worry ... do not be afraid. I will not leave you alone."

After supper, Jesus went to a garden called Gethsemane. He took Peter, James, and John with

Him. While He was there praying, one of His own friends—a man called Judas—went to the authorities. He told them where Jesus was, and brought soldiers to the garden.

Jesus saw them coming; so did Peter; so did James and John. The three disciples were terribly frightened. They ran away. Jesus was left by Himself.

He let His enemies take Him prisoner.

Jesus' enemies beat Him with sticks. They slapped Him, spat upon Him, and laughed at Him. His enemies turned people against Him. The next morning they led Jesus to the Roman governor, Pontius Pilate, and accused Him of many things.

Jesus had done no wrong, but He was sentenced to death.

They put Him on a wooden cross . . . they drove nails through His hands and feet . . .

Jesus was crucified.

Before He died, Jesus prayed, "Father, forgive them; for they know not what they do."

A few friends took Jesus' body down from the cross and buried it in a tomb in a garden. They rolled a heavy stone before the door and went away.

Jesus' enemies thought they had won.

The disciples hid in Jerusalem. All their hopes, and dreams, seemed to die with Jesus, on the cross.

A day went by, an empty day; and a night, a long night. Then, Mary Magdalene, who loved Jesus, went to the garden where He was buried. Two other women were with her. They walked slowly, sorrowfully, through the darkness of the garden. The grass was wet under their feet, soaking the hems of their long robes. They moved

silently, but their coming startled the sleepy birds into song.

Dawn was very near.

Soon, soon now . . . it would be light.

They came to the tomb. They stopped in wonder and amazement.

The great stone was rolled away.

The tomb was empty.

Jesus was not there.

An angel, bright messenger of God, stood near the door. He spoke to them:

"Do not be afraid. You come seeking Jesus, who was crucified. But He is not here! He is risen! Go quickly, tell His disciples that Jesus lives!"

The women turned to run. They took a few steps, and stopped.

Jesus stood on the path before them! He was alive again!

They fell at His feet; they touched Him.

"Hurry to my friends," Jesus said. "Tell them to go to Galilee. I will meet them there."

Breakfast on the Shore

AFTER Mary Magdelene told the disciples she had
seen Jesus in the garden, Peter, with his brother
Andrew and some of the other disciples, went
home to Galilee. They went back to their boats
and their nets, to the wide, deep lake where they
had first met Jesus.

They longed to see Him again. Until He came to them, they would wait, and work.

"I am going fishing," said Peter, late one afternoon.

The others agreed to go with him. Climbing aboard their boat, they pulled out onto the lake.

The sun went down; the moon rode across the sky. Time and again the men cast their net into the water; time and again they drew it up. All night long they fished, but they caught nothing. The net was always empty.

Toward morning the discouraged fishermen brought the boat in close to shore. It had been a long night. They were tired, hungry, and cold.

And then, just as the sun burst from behind a hill, Jesus stood on the beach. He waved to them and called, "Have you any fish?"

In the early light Jesus' friends did not recognize Him. "No," they shouted back. "No luck. . . . We've caught nothing all night."

"Throw your net on the right side of the boat," Jesus called across the water. "You will catch some fish then."

The fishermen did as He said. Suddenly the net was so heavy with fish they could hardly hold it. One of them looked again at the man on the shore. "It is the Lord!" he said, his face shining with joy.

Simon Peter dropped his hold on the net. With a great shout he dove over the side of the boat into the water. He did not wait for the others; he swam for shore, letting them come after in the boat, dragging the net behind them!

When the rest of the fishermen reached land, they found a charcoal fire burning, with a few fish cooking and bread warming beside the coals. Jesus said, "Bring some of the fish you have just caught." Peter went back on board the boat and hauled the net ashore. He picked out several large fish and brought them to the fire.

"Now," Jesus said, "come and have breakfast." The fish sizzled among the coals, turning crisp and brown. Jesus took the warm bread and broke it into pieces, giving some to each of His friends. When the fish was cooked, He divided it up in the same way, and they all ate.

Jesus and the men He loved sat around the fire in the early morning. No one said to Him, "Who are you?" They knew it was the risen Lord.

Jesus Sends His Spirit

In the days after the first Easter, Jesus often appeared to His friends. "Before many days go by," He promised, "I will send you my Spirit. When that happens, you will be able to go out as my apostles—my messengers—to tell people everywhere what you know of me."

Soon after Jesus said this, His disciples saw Him no more.

They waited expectantly, meeting every day to eat, to pray, to talk over old times. They thought of the things Jesus had done when He was with them, the stories He told, and the places they had been together. They remembered the day in Galilee when Jesus came walking down to the shore to call them away from their nets; Jericho, and

Zacchaeus up in the tree; Bartimaeus, who because he believed could see again. In memory they
heard the voice of Jesus as He taught them to pray
. . . "Our Father . . . in heaven . . . Thy will be
done . . . " They talked of their last supper with
Him, and the terrible day when Jesus was killed.
But most of all, they spoke of the joy of the morning when Mary Magdalene had found the empty
tomb, and had come to tell them that Jesus was
alive again.

Then one morning, when the disciples were all together, an extraordinary thing happened.

A sound like the rushing of a mighty wind suddenly filled the house, roaring about their ears. As the disciples sat, stunned by the noise, they saw what appeared to be little tongues of fire over the head of every person in the room.

In a moment, the sound of the wind was gone, the tongues of fire had disappeared. But the disciples knew what had happened. *The Spirit of Jesus had come to them.* He had kept His promise. Outwardly, the disciples looked the same, but inwardly, from that moment forward, they were changed men.

Now at that time there were many men in Jerusalem from countries far away. Hearing the shouts of the disciples, they came running to see what the excitement was about. Other people came, too. They listened to the apostles, completely bewildered. It seemed to make no difference what country they came from, they could understand every word!

"What has happened?" they asked in amazement. "These men are all from Galilee. How can they suddenly talk so that all of us can understand them?"

Then Peter spoke. He knew what he must do and how it must be done. He was sure of himself. "Listen to me!" he shouted. "Listen to me! I speak of Jesus of Nazareth, who was crucified. *Jesus is not dead!* We know this. We have seen Him! It is His Spirit that you see and hear working in us today. God made Jesus the Lord of all the world."

Hearing these words, many people cried, "But what can we do? Tell us what to do. . . ."

Peter answered them. "Come and be baptized in Jesus' Name," he said, "and you, too, will receive His Spirit. Jesus' promise is to you, and to your children; to everyone, even those far away. Believe in Him, and you will be saved."

On that day, many people were baptized, and became followers of Jesus. They joined the apostles to share the work and the joy of all they did.

As the days and weeks and years rolled by, the number of Jesus' followers continued to grow; spreading out to the farthest corners of the world, carrying the good news of our Lord Jesus Christ to all people; carrying it to *you*.